The FATHER!

God's Cure for Loneliness and Rejection

MARTIN OSSEI

authorHOUSE®

AuthorHouse™ UK
1663 Liberty Drive
Bloomington, IN 47403 USA
www.authorhouse.co.uk
Phone: 0800.197.4150

Scripture taken from the New King James Version®. Copyright © 1982 by Thomas Nelson. Used by permission. All rights reserved.

Scripture quotations marked NLT are taken from the Holy Bible, New Living Translation, copyright © 1996, 2004, 2007. Used by permission of Tyndale House Publishers, Inc. Carol Stream, Illinois 60188. All rights reserved. Website

Published by AuthorHouse 10/18/2018

ISBN: 978-1-5462-9961-5 (sc)
ISBN: 978-1-5462-9960-8 (e)

Print information available on the last page.

CONTENTS

{ FOREWORD }

FATHERHOOD is a gift of God to provide leadership to all of creation. Without a father, you are bound to face loneliness and rejection. There is no child who does not have a father. Imperfect man has abandoned this great gift and brought great suffering to many.

This book provides an in-depth exposition on fatherhood as God intended and hopefully will bring deliverance to many who have suffered from the absence of a father. It looks at the father-son relationship between God and man and from man to generations after him.

This book is biblically based and will provide refreshing restoration to a lot of people suffering from loneliness and rejection. Pastor Martin has written this book in his characteristic beautiful, flowing, easy to read style. Enjoy the rich wisdom in this book and recommend it to a friend.

I have known and worked with Pastor Martin Ossei for over two decades and can affirm that the fatherhood he has revealed in this book is something he lives and provides in his family, ministry and community. He provides a true man of God's perspective on Fatherhood. He reveals God as a doting father ready to bless his children with the power of fatherhood.

May your heart be lifted up and filled with the knowledge of Fatherhood – from God to man, and from man to the sons of men as you enjoy this book.

Rev. Kofi Nyarko
Associate Pastor
Joyhouse London

A PERSONAL JOURNEY

There is a popular saying that 'we come into this world alone and exit it alone.' In other words, every person has an individual part to play in this drama called life. Your life is unique in the midst of many look-alikes. The United Nations Children's Fund (UNICEF), a United Nations Programme to aid education and the health of children and mothers in developing countries, estimates that an average of 353,000 babies are born every day in the world yet each child is different. Even multiple birth babies have their individual identities. The current highest record of multiple babies is octuplets (8 babies) and each of these babies have their individual identity and personality.

Each person on planet earth has therefore been wonderfully and uniquely crafted. I use the word "crafted" as of a deliberate product of a craftsman. The nature of humans is too sophisticated to have happened by any kind of scientific or historical accident. There is overwhelming evidence that a superior being to man deliberately and meticulously crafted man. The Bible tells us that God made man. He took his time to wonderfully make each one of us. King David clearly expresses this truth in his prophetic song to God:

"For You formed my inward parts;
You covered me in my mother's womb.
I will praise You, for I am fearfully and wonderfully made;
Marvelous are Your works,
And that my soul knows very well.
My frame was not hidden from You,
When I was made in secret,
And skilfully wrought in the lowest parts of the earth.
Your eyes saw my substance, being yet unformed.
And in Your book they all were written,
The days fashioned for me,
When as yet there were none of them.
How precious also are Your thoughts to me, O God!

How great is the sum of them!
If I should count them, they would be more in number than the sand;
When I awake, I am still with You." Psalm 139:13-18

David's psalm above, presents the picture of an artist in the process of creating an art piece. He takes us into the mind of the artist, from the conception of the idea, describing its purpose through to its creation. He even describes the sentiment of deep love of the creator towards his creation. David was describing the moment of the creation of man by God. David was inspired, through his psalms, to give us glimpses of the nature and mind of God. This extract from the psalm is a narration of the history of creation through prophetic song.

It is impossible to know our purpose as humans on this earth, till we know where we have come from. Every creator has a purpose for his creation. David's song clearly tells us that God has written the days purposed for us in his book. To be ignorant of his plan for our lives is too expensive a price to pay. Without revelation, there are no barriers. If you don't have a clear destination, you would not know when you arrive. You are on a journey but never seem to arrive. Your journey could be a lonely path of endless toil with no light at the end of the tunnel. Helplessness and frustration will lead to a sense of rejection and self-loathing.

This book delivers God's answer to the terrorising twins of Rejection and Loneliness. Humans are the object of God's love. He did not wonderfully create us to live a life of loneliness and rejection. The source of man's troubles has always been his ignorance. Therefore, you must know the purpose for which you were created.

In the following chapters, we are going to look at the gift of a 'Father,' which God has made available to every human being. If you were born, then you have a father. It takes a father to make a baby. You may not know your father, but every birth is the product of a father's seed.

The incarnated Jesus Christ is the only person who lived in the flesh without a human father. Yet his birth, life and ministry were anchored in an ever-present giant of a father who could not be ignored. When you met Jesus, you met his father. He told his disciples that when they see him, they are looking at his father; that he was one with his father. He attributed all his knowledge, words, actions and authority to his Father.

The role of a father is to be the source of knowledge, provision and protection.

Many fathers have taken the responsibility of fatherhood lightly and robbed their children of true knowledge, provision and protection. Many in the world are going through life like sheep without a shepherd. The absence of a father is the absence of leadership and guidance. Our society today is confused because of the absence of true leadership. The world is crying out for real fathers.

The purpose of this book is to restore the gift of fatherhood back to the world. This book will make fathers out of men and boys. It will bring understanding of fatherhood to women and girls and facilitate their roles as mothers. This book will bring hope to those who feel fatherless, rejected and lonely.

Jesus Christ brought the extraordinary message of God as his father and also that God was ready to be a father to all who would accept him as father. Most of his countrymen, the Jews, in his day, could not readily accept this message because to make God your father was to bring God too close for comfort. They called the message of Jesus Christ, blasphemy because to make yourself a son of God was to declare that you are like God. They preferred to have Abraham as their father since he was human just like them. However, Abraham was long dead and could not teach them everlasting truth, provide for them or protect them. God was offering to be a father to them, but they preferred to stick to their tradition handed down by their predecessors because that was easier to handle.

This offer of God to be a father to everyone still stands. My prayer for you is that, as you read this revelation from the heart of God, you would not be distracted by past disappointments of rejection. Rather, you will fall into the warm embracing arms of a father who is waiting for you. Age is no barrier. Whether you are a hundred years or 3 hours old, everyone needs a father. Enjoy being fathered and becoming a father.

I thank my wife and co-labourer, Catherine, for her contribution and invaluable support in the writing of this book. I am also grateful to my editor, Mrs. Betty Smith, for proof-reading and ensuring that this book is readable. Enjoy reading.

CHAPTER 1

THE FATHER AND THE SON

One of the most challenged truths of Christianity is 'Jesus Christ as the Son of God.' When he walked on the earth as man, the religious people of the day saw him as a blasphemer. They hated him and plotted to kill him for he called himself the son of God. How could a mere man call himself the son of God?

In the world today, there is still disagreement about who Jesus Christ really is. Some say he may be the son of God but cannot be God. Others dismiss his claim to be the son of God by arguing that God cannot have children as he has no wife. Jesus Christ, however, made the fact that he was the son of God, the centre of his message. It was clearly the foundation for his legitimacy and authority.

Everything on this earth has its origins from something else and is connected to its source through genes and physical resemblance. Only God has no beginning and no end. He is the source of all things. It is only God's word that can create something out of nothing, and he created the 'Heavens and the Earth' out of nothing. He commanded humans, animals, and plants to produce after their own kind. Humans would give birth to humans, animals to animals and plants to plants. God commanded them to 'Be fruitful and multiply.'

To be fruitful is to produce after your own kind. Humans, animals and plants are to multiply by producing after their own kind. It is important to note from the scripture below that God commanded the earth to produce plants and then commanded the plants and animals to produce after their own kind.

"Then God said, "Let the earth bring forth grass, the herb that yields seed, and the fruit tree that yields fruit according to its kind, whose seed is in itself, on the earth"; and it was so. And the earth brought forth grass, the herb that yields seed according to its kind, and the tree that yields fruit, whose seed is in

itself according to its kind. And God saw that it was good." Genesis 1:11-12

"Then God said, "Let the waters abound with an abundance of living creatures, and let birds fly above the earth across the face of the firmament of the heavens." So God created great sea creatures and every living thing that moves, with which the waters abounded, according to their kind, and every winged bird according to its kind. And God saw that it was good. And God blessed them, saying, "Be fruitful and multiply, and fill the waters in the seas, and let birds multiply on the earth." So the evening and the morning were the fifth day.

Then God said, "Let the earth bring forth the living creature according to its kind: cattle and creeping thing and beast of the earth, each according to its kind"; and it was so. And God made the beast of the earth according to its kind, cattle according to its kind, and everything that creeps on the earth according to its kind. And God saw that it was good." Genesis 1:20-26

When Jesus appeared on the streets of Galilee and Jerusalem, he differed from the religious leaders of the time. The religious leaders of the time based their relationship with God on covenants made with God through their ancestors, Abraham and Moses. Jesus, on the other hand, came declaring that God was his father. Jesus was releasing, through his person, direct flow of spiritual milk from heaven.

You can't get better than the Son of God, standing in front of you with evidence of ever-flowing life from His heavenly Father.

On the other hand, there were religious Pharisees and Scribes who acted as representatives of God, presiding over religious activities and enforcing the 'laws of God' many of which were man-made. These religious men were the so-called 'men of God.' They spoke for and mediated between God and man. They took their roles seriously and zealously proclaimed and prosecuted 'God's law.' They could give orders for people to be killed or punished in the name of God. They bestowed honour on men on behalf of God. The source of their authority was centuries old covenant that their ancestors had with God. The terms of this covenant had suffered the battering and modifications of age. These were religious men who wore the robes 'prescribed' by God and claimed to hear from God.

Every now and then, there would appear Prophets who claimed to speak for God. Some of them were genuine prophets, sent by God, who moved in supernatural power. They would deliver instructions from God and make predictions of the future which came to pass. These men were feared and revered and they could bring whole cities to their knees. There were prophets of such high reputation, that mighty kings would not make a move without consulting them.

None of these 'powerful' men and women of God ever made a claim of God being their father. To make such a claim would be the height of arrogance and they dared not. They believed that "God was an all-powerful creator and master of the heavens and earth and they were mere mortal and servants, walking the earth as slaves of fate." The calling and assignment of God placed on their lives was an uncomfortable burden even to the genuine prophets. Other so-called men of God who occupied their positions through lineage or manipulation were scared to draw close to God. Though they exploited other people with the title and perks of their offices, they were afraid to draw near to God because of the feeling of guilt that sin always carries.

When Jesus appeared on the scene telling the people that he had come from God and that God was his father, they accused him of being possessed by the devil. What they did not know was that God had always been desperate for children. **The Israelites saw God as a master, but God desired for sons.** God did not just create the world. He carefully considered everything before speaking them into being. Everything God created has a purpose.

Before God created man, we hear him think aloud in Genesis 1:26:

"Then God said, "Let Us make man in Our image, according to Our likeness; let them have dominion over the fish of the sea, over the birds of the air, and over the cattle, over all the earth and over every creeping thing that creeps on the earth." So God created man in His own image; in the image of God

He created him; male and female He created them. Then God blessed them, and God said to them, "Be fruitful and multiply; fill the earth and subdue it; have dominion over the fish of the sea, over the birds of the air, and over every living thing that moves on the earth." Genesis 1:26-28

Creating man in his own image and likeness, was God's first attempt at having sons of his own. Man was created after God had created everything else on earth. He created man in his own image and likeness. Genesis 2:7 says he breathed the breath of life into man's nostrils and man became a living being. This was God's own special life breathed into man. The animals and plants were breathing, but that was not the breath of God. By breathing into Adam, God did not only have a son who looked and behaved like him, but he also had God's own breath running through his nostrils. **Everyone born of God has the breath of God running through their nostrils.**

God gave man freewill to do what he pleases. He endowed humans with the privilege of choice. We could even choose to be with God or to be without God.

Unfortunately, the first man, Adam, chose to separate himself from God through disobedience. This separation from God is the source of the curse that has hung over man all these years. It has been the source of the loneliness and sense of rejection that man has felt all through the ages.

Man was not created to be fatherless. To be fatherless is to be headless, visionless and without protection. Man stepped out of God's light into darkness and needed to generate his own light. From that point on, man has made many efforts to enhance his existence, but all attempts fall short of the light of God. **Loneliness and rejection are the resulting feelings of anyone separated from their natural relationship with their father.**

It would have been a tragedy if man's separation from his creator had not been remedied. Fortunately, no cunning of the devil or foolishness of man could distract God from his purpose for man. He was going to have sons, and nothing would stop that.

Through the disobedience of the first man, Adam, God's fatherhood of all humans had been stopped. Adam had become the father of mankind hence when he separated himself from God his father, we his children, got separated too. The tragedy to all of us, his descendants, was that Adam was ignorant and could not pass on any knowledge to us. He had removed himself from his source of knowledge, God. He had no protection, and he had to struggle to provide for himself. It became a case of the blind leading the blind into a ditch.

The world is in a ditch because the fatherhood of God was truncated. The important role of a knowledgeable father in the affairs of men had been lost. Immorality and despair abound because true knowledge is not being passed on from fathers to children. Well-meaning fathers cannot protect or provide for their children because they have no power source and their earthly knowledge is too weak against the menacing power of Satan. Weak fathers are no match for the wild, out-of-control economic and social systems of the world powered by Satan himself.

We thank God for his eternally loving nature and all-encompassing power because, at the appointed time in history, He sent his son Jesus Christ on the scene with a new message of hope. "God, the father, is desperate to have his family back." He wants the whole world back to their original roots. He has come as a father to rescue his children who have been fearfully and wonderfully made.

Jesus' mission on earth was to announce the return of Father God for his children; to pay the price of death for our sins, and create a highway back home to God.

The father-child relationship is foundational to God's creation plan. Jesus Christ came to restore this original plan of God which Adam had lost.

The father's seed is what produces fruit. God's desire is that his seed would have run through the first man continuously to the last child ever born. In Ezekiel chapter 47, Ezekiel sees a vision of a river flowing from under the altar in the temple. This water of life brought God's glory wherever it went. The altar represents God, and the river represent the life flow from God. Everything that was in the path of this flow received new life, freshness and fruitfulness. Everything that was not in the path was stale, salty and dead.

Adam stopped the flow from God the father, and so Jesus came to restore this flow. Jesus became the new connection to a very willing father. The apostle John writes this about Jesus:

"He was in the world, and the world was made through Him, and the world did not know Him. He came to His own, and His own did not receive Him. But as many as received Him, to them He gave the right to become children of God, to those who believe in His name: who were born, not of blood, nor of the will of the flesh, nor of the will of man, but of God." John 1:10-13

A father-son relationship is much cosier than a master-servant relationship. **If Adam had not broken his father-son relationship with God, there would have been no place for a master-servant relationship in the world.** The latter is the product of the survival mentality which the absence of a father brought. The struggle of life made man self-centred and competitive. Competition breeds the need to show superiority. Thus, man became ruthless in his quest to be superior and respected and was ready to enslave or kill for personal survival.

Jesus Christ brought the restoration of the father-son relationship between God and man. Therefore, connection to the Founding Father has been re-established and once more, wisdom is flowing from the ultimate father – God. True fatherhood is now possible, hence real fathers are rising who are imparting the grace and truth of God to their children, seeking to patiently release what they have received from God to their children. There are also sons and daughters who are gratefully receiving from their fathers and who honour their parents. There are many sons who are receiving the life flow from God through their fathers and are maturing into fathers themselves, ready to impart godly seed to their own children.

THERE ARE TWO KINGDOMS

There are two kingdoms operating on this earth. One is the kingdom of God, and the other is the kingdom of the world. The kingdom of the world prides itself on independent knowledge or knowledge derived from the study of our environment (Science). The kingdom of the world thrives on the intelligence of man.

The kingdom of God, on the other hand, is solidly founded on God's Word and knowledge, handed down through fathers. Therefore, the role of fathers is indispensable in the kingdom of God.

Whilst scientific scholars, thinkers and people with good imagination and drive are the gurus of the kingdom of the world, fathers are the repositories and imparters of knowledge in the kingdom of God. The world's knowledge is changing every day as new research unravel new discoveries. There is no stability in the knowledge of the world. One day, you are told the yolk of an egg is healthier than the white. The next day, this knowledge is 'corrected' making the white healthier. These disagreements often end up in knowledge wars with entrenched positions where further research is aimed at defending mind-sets. Human frailty undermines the genuineness of so-called expert knowledge. Any knowledge without a solid foundation is bound to crumble. That is why the kingdom of the world is descending into greater confusion. World knowledge is increasing every day, but the world is never coming to knowledge. The gap between questions and answers is widening. The more the world finds out, the less it knows.

I encourage you to become a citizen of the kingdom of God if you are not already one. Your citizenship makes you a son of God with all the benefits of being the son and heir to the creator and master of the universe. **Everyone is automatically part of the kingdom of the world, but it takes a deliberate choice to be part of the kingdom of God.**

The kingdom of God is founded on the love of God demonstrated by the death of His son, Jesus Christ on the Cross of Calvary. This is a sacrifice Jesus undertook as payment for the sins of the world to pave the way for all people to return to God and enjoy the benefits of a true father. This is a covenant of blood. If God is ready to pay the price of death for your deliverance, then prepare yourself for a true love affair when you make him your father.

CHAPTER 2

DO YOU KNOW WHO I AM?

"Do you know who I am?" is a rhetorical question often asked to reveal identity. The speaker would be asking for recognition based on his identity. It is sometimes used in veiled threats: "If you knew who I was, you would check yourself." Identity is very central to our own self-esteem and how people receive us. A member of the royal family is likely to receive special courtesies. People respond to a celebrity or a law enforcement officer according to their identity.

The world gives special respect to certain people more than they do others. This act of discrimination is mostly fuelled by standards set by men. Some of these standards could be so blatantly unfair that it exposes the ignorance behind our choices. If you disrespect someone for their disability or skin colour, you are operating out of ignorance.

In a 'survival of the fittest' world, we struggle to diminish others in order to feel superior. We will bully or deceive to gain respect. A sense of superiority makes us feel more powerful. This competition for respect can lead to such negative sentiments as hatred and murder. There are people who are ready to face ruin just for the warped satisfaction of seeing their competitors ruined. This brutal attitude is borne out of a lack of true identity. Many tend to want to create an artificial identity for themselves. The multi-billion cosmetic industry is one of the main beneficiaries of this craving. As someone rightly put it: "Drunkenness does not solve the question. It makes you forget the question only for it to pop up again when you are sober." If you want to permanently forget the question, then you must stay drunk permanently which may produce more serious consequences than the question.

By God's grace, there is an answer to this identity question. You do not need to stay drunk. **God,**

who is our creator, is the only one who knows our true identity. Your true identity is great. You are the son or daughter of God himself if you choose to be.

As descendants of Adam, we have inherited some bad traits of Adam. The consequence of sin is death and fear. Sinful Adam has passed on death and fear to his descendants. Inheriting the identity of Adam has reduced people to a life of fear. Fear makes people defensive and self-conscious. Selfishness is the order of the day in the land of fear.

Scripture tells us that man was created for the purpose of dominion. Our identity could be found in God's intent, clearly expressed in Genesis 1:26-28:

"Then God said, "Let Us make man in Our image, according to Our likeness; let them have dominion over the fish of the sea, over the birds of the air, and over the cattle, over all the earth and over every creeping thing that creeps on the earth." So God created man in His own image; in the image of God He created him; male and female He created them. Then God blessed them, and God said to them, "Be

fruitful and multiply; fill the earth and subdue it; have dominion over the fish of the sea, over the birds of the air, and over every living thing that moves on the earth."

The only way created man could know his true identity was through revelation from the creator. When man separated himself from his creator, he had separated himself from the knowledge of himself. Man, therefore, gave himself a new false identity based on his perceptions influenced by his surroundings. Man had become like the eagle in the proverbial 'Eagle who grew up among chickens' story. The story goes like this:

'An orphaned eaglet was brought up among chickens and always thought it was a chicken. She admired other eagles glide by gracefully and wished she could be like the eagles. What she didn't know was that she was an eagle. She continued to peck the ground for food. The other chickens, who were no wiser discouraged her from the fanciful thought of wanting to be an eagle as she was just a different looking chicken.' This eagle died a chicken's death going through her existence with a false identity.

Tragically, that has been the plight of man without God. The identity of man has been diminished to the point of man being identified as part of the animal species. Humans are classified by some scholars as mammals in the sub category of 'primates' and 'great apes.' It is no wonder many humans feel worthless and depressed. Many humans are striving to be 'humans' but remain victims of ignorance. When you walk in a diminished identity, you strive to be what you already are.

Satan was able to deceive Adam and Eve to desire power they already had. He had whispered a false identity in their ear and sent them on a fool's errand of disobeying God. All through scripture, when the people of God separated themselves from God, they became vulnerable and easy prey for the enemy.

In Judges 6, Israel, a nation God had sworn to protect, had become easy plunder for their enemies, the Midianites. This was because they had turned their backs on God. They would work hard to produce crops, but the Midianites would come at the time of harvest and steal their harvest. God in his mercy decides to intervene and chooses Gideon as his man to lead Israel in this war against Midian. The conversation between God's angel and Gideon is recorded in Judges 6:12-16:

And the Angel of the Lord appeared to him, and said to him, "The Lord is with you, you mighty man of valor!"

Gideon said to Him, "O my lord, if the Lord is with us, why then has all this happened to us? And where are all His miracles which our fathers told us about, saying, 'Did not the Lord bring us up from Egypt?' But now the Lord has forsaken us and delivered us into the hands of the Midianites."

Then the Lord turned to him and said, "Go in this might of yours, and you shall save Israel from the hand of the Midianites. Have I not sent you?"

So he said to Him, "O my Lord, how can I save Israel? Indeed my clan is the weakest in Manasseh, and I am the least in my father's house."

And the Lord said to him, "Surely I will be with you, and you shall defeat the Midianites as one man."

Gideon's true identity was 'a mighty man of valour.' That was how the angel of God addressed him. It is obvious from the extract above that he saw his identity as completely opposite to how God saw him. He saw his clan as the weakest and himself as weakest in his father's house. No wonder he was hiding from his enemies. God propped Gideon up in his new identity. Eventually, Gideon, with God 'in his face,' walked in his true identity and led Israel to defeat the Midianites. **God cannot produce weaklings. Partnership with God produces a new identity anchored in the strength of God.**

A born-again believer is born of God, with the identity of a true child of God. It is this same identity that Jesus walked in when he walked the earth. It is with this identity that Jesus displayed the power of heaven on earth. Being the son of God is not just a religious cliché. It is truth.

He was in the world, and the world was made through Him, and the world did not know Him. He came to His own, and His own did not receive Him. But as many as received Him, to them He gave the right to become children of God, to those who believe in His name: who were born, not of blood, nor of the will of the flesh, nor of the will of man, but of God. John 1:10-13

If you are a prince and you don't know it, you cannot possibly live like a prince.

What is your identity?

Another way of asking this question is: Who are you? Our perception of who we are could be entirely different from who we really are. The knowledge of who we really are can transform our thinking dramatically.

Science has made huge advancement in the field of genetics in recent years. Through sample tissues of the body, we are able to correctly predict the ancestry of people. This shows that there is a line of identification running from our fathers through us to our children. To be dislodged from this identity flow is to lose your real identity. When you don't walk in your real identity, you walk in a false identity.

Every man has been created in the image and likeness of God. Unfortunately, many do not know this. God created humans to relate to Him as father. Our first ancestors rejected God as a father. They, therefore, did not enjoy the cushion and the knowledge of God the father. Through the generations, children have had to depend on the knowledge of their ancestors acquired through learning and experience. This worldly knowledge started from Adam and Eve. Having been cut off from God through disobedience, they survived on what they remembered from their time with God and what they learnt through trial and error as they plodded on in life.

From the time of the creation of the world, because of the separation between Father God and the rest of creation, man has lived by human knowledge primarily. Scripture reveals to us that, God has made several interventions to reveal himself to man.

In Genesis 12, God makes a promise to Abraham. If Abraham would obey God, God promised to bless Abraham with abundance like the stars in the sky. God could say that because he created the stars. What Abraham had to do was to come in the opposite direction to Adam. Adam walked away from God in the direction of the world. He walked away from a father's wisdom into a beautiful world with no knowledge of how to operate or survive in that world. God called Abraham away from the world to a designated place chosen by God. God promised to supply every desire of Abraham's heart and more:

"Now the Lord had said to Abram:
"Get out of your country,
From your family
And from your father's house,
To a land that I will show you.
I will make you a great nation;
I will bless you
And make your name great;
And you shall be a blessing.
I will bless those who bless you,
And I will curse him who curses you;
And in you all the families of the earth shall be blessed." Genesis 12:1-3

Abraham obeyed God and became a covenant friend of God. God demonstrated his wisdom and power through Abraham. All Israel are proud to call Abraham their father because Abraham's covenant was their covenant. **Children are partakers of their father's covenant because it is expected that the blessing would flow naturally from fathers to children.**

Fathers must not withhold the flow of the blessing to the children, and children must not separate themselves from the father's flow through disobedience. **Your identity is from your father. You are who your father is.** The nation of Israel has always prided itself on its special relationship with the one true God. Their confidence is solely based on God's covenant with Abraham. God's promises to Abraham were to Abraham and his descendants.

CHAPTER 3

MISTAKEN IDENTITY

In a recent DNA experiment to determine the ancestry of 67 people from different parts of the world, they were all found to be ignorant of who they really were. One English guy who did not like Germans because of the world wars found out that he was part German. Some of them found out that they were blood relatives to people they had scoffed at. The purpose of this experiment was to generate understanding and tolerance between cultures. It was clear that the revelation of their true identity was going to change the attitudes of the participants. Interestingly, Belgian DNA researchers posted in 2010 that the infamous Adolf Hitler had Jewish and African blood in him. What difference it could have made to this champion of the 'superior' German race who killed many Jews and Africans, referring to them as animals!

One of the main themes in scripture was God's fulfilment of his promise to Abraham to give him the land of Canaan. He had multiplied the descendants of Abraham as promised. They had become a nation. He had taken them from under the nose of the most powerful king of the time on a journey to the promised land. On this journey, God had demonstrated his authority as God through many supernatural signs. As they drew closer to the promised land, God directs them to go and check out the land they were destined to inherit. God wanted them to have a feel of the goodness of His promise.

Twelve spies were despatched to check the land, and they came back with confirmation that the land was as great as God had said. However, ten of the twelve spies were heartbroken because there were giants in the land and, in their own eyes, it was impossible to occupy the land. This was their report:

"Then they told him, and said: "We went to the land where you sent us. It truly flows with milk

and honey, and this is its fruit. Nevertheless the people who dwell in the land are strong; the cities are fortified and very large; moreover we saw the descendants of Anak there. The Amalekites dwell in the land of the South; the Hittites, the Jebusites, and the Amorites dwell in the mountains; and the Canaanites dwell by the sea and along the banks of the Jordan."

Then Caleb quieted the people before Moses, and said, "Let us go up at once and take possession, for we are well able to overcome it."

But the men who had gone up with him said, "We are not able to go up against the people, for they are stronger than we." And they gave the children of Israel a bad report of the land which they had spied out, saying, "The land through which we have gone as spies is a land that devours its inhabitants, and all the people whom we saw in it are men of great stature. There we saw the giants (the descendants of Anak came from the giants); and we were like grasshoppers in our own sight, and so we were in their sight."

Numbers 13:27-33

Their fear was produced by the perception they had of their own identity, as expressed in the last sentence of the scripture above: *"We were like grasshoppers in our own sight, and so we were in their sight."* When they saw the giants, their self-image was reduced to that of a grasshopper. They were so overtaken by their mistaken self-image that they thought everyone else saw them as grasshoppers.

They had forgotten about the God who made the promise of giving the land to them; the God who had demonstrated his authority to them through wonderful signs and miracles as they journeyed to the promised land. If they had remembered the God who made the promise, they would not have been afraid of the giants. Joshua and Caleb, the only two of the twelve who knew their true identity, did not see themselves as grasshoppers, but as giant destroyers and occupants of the land flowing with milk and honey. They were confident in the ability of the one who made the promise, not in their own ability. Daniel 11:32b says, "*the people who know their God shall be strong, and carry out great exploits.*"

May you be like Joshua and Caleb who did not look at their own stature but the stature of God, who promised the land. The ten fearful spies with mistaken self-identity died in the desert without enjoying the land of milk and honey. Joshua and Caleb, who put their trust in God, entered the promised land with full confidence and possessed the land.

God's plan for us is to be His sons. If we make the decision to come to him, he wants us to know we are his sons. He receives us as his sons. He is the best father anyone could have. Without the security of the trusted position of a son, we are likely to walk in a false identity of loneliness and vulnerability. A strong father does not want weak children. **Children of God who have a weak self-image are rebels walking in disobedience.** As the father is, so is the son.

Your father is the custodian of your true identity. If you are born of God, then only God knows your true identity. We must believe who he says we are. God does not see you as weak because God cannot give birth to weak sons. God is strong and gives birth to strong sons.

The world sees things differently from God. The world would normally judge by what they see and hear with their natural senses. The spies who went to Canaan saw the occupiers of the land as giants who were physically too large to defeat. These God-sent spies, therefore, saw themselves as grasshoppers unable to take the promised land. They measured strength by physical stature.

The weakness of humans is apparent when they are separated from God. The first man Adam freely walked and talked with God till he was deceived into disobeying God. This disobedience which led to separation from God, made Adam feel so dirty and unworthy in his own eyes that he hid himself from God. This has been the plight of man without God till now. There is a desire to be with God, but a feeling of unworthiness makes it impossible to approach Him.

It would take God, becoming a man and invading the hide-out of man to break through this crippling fear of man. Jesus lived as a man and faced all the temptations of man but never fell into sin. He faced every battle and temptation of the devil but never lost his self-dignity to the extent of disobeying God. Scripture tells us that He took on the sin of the world and died from this burden of sin. He was made sin for the whole world so that he could reconcile the world to God:

"For He made Him who knew no sin to be sin for us, that we might become the righteousness of God in Him." 2 Corinthians 5:21

CHAPTER 4

WALK IN YOUR TRUE IDENTITY

"For as many as are led by the Spirit of God, these are sons of God. For you did not receive the spirit of bondage again to fear, but you received the Spirit of adoption by whom we cry out, "Abba, Father." The Spirit Himself bears witness with our spirit that we are children of God, and if children, then heirs— heirs of God and joint heirs with Christ, if indeed we suffer with Him, that we may also be glorified together." Romans 8:14-17

When Jesus was put to death on the Cross in Jerusalem some two thousand years ago, there was nothing extraordinary about this execution. The ruling Romans had used this form of punishment hundreds of times before Jesus Christ. In fact, on the day of the crucifixion of Jesus Christ, two criminals were crucified with Him. The crucifixion of Jesus Christ, however, was not one that the Romans or anyone else was going to forget easily. Almighty God himself had orchestrated this death.

This was no ordinary death. The sun took away its light on the day, plunging the earth into darkness. The dreaded, heavy temple curtain that separated the people from the presence of God was ripped into two from top to bottom. God himself ripped it from his abode in heaven. There was an earthquake and rocks were split apart. Mighty impregnable rocks were split into two. Dead men were raised from the dead as graves burst open. The death of Jesus Christ shook heaven and earth. There was the display of the power of God.

This was no fun fair. There was a purpose to this display of power. God was announcing to the world, the creation of his new family. Big brother Jesus paid the price for sin which had separated us from God. He stands in the place of the curtain of separation. He stands between God and the world to reconcile the world to God. Jesus, through his death, has torn down the wall of separation between man and God.

He now invites 'whosoever' desires, to enjoy a father-son relationship with God through him (Jesus). His sacrifice on the Cross of Calvary was thorough. Heaven received this sacrifice with satisfaction and confirmed its acceptance with mighty signs in heaven and on earth. Jesus rose from the dead to show that death has no power over the Son. He has given this power to become sons of God to as many as would receive him.

"He was in the world, and the world was made through Him, and the world did not know Him. He came to His own, and His own did not receive Him. But as many as received Him, to them He gave the right to become children of God, to those who believe in His name: who were born, not of blood, nor of the will of the flesh, nor of the will of man, but of God." John 1:10-13

This gives every person born on this earth an opportunity to belong to the family of God. The only qualification is to receive Jesus Christ into your life. You receive Jesus Christ by accepting him for who he is; that is, by acknowledging the price of death he paid for the reconciliation of the world to God, His resurrection from the dead and his Lordship over all creation.

When we become part of the family of God, we become heirs of God. We become partakers of his glory. This is the identity of everyone who is in Christ. Before the death and resurrection of Jesus Christ, scripture tells us that we had all sinned and fallen short of the glory of God (Romans 3:23). Our true identity had been compromised by sin. We sought to carve out an identity for ourselves. A 'respectable' identity would be one that measured to people's expectation. We, therefore, played to the gallery. The cheers from the gallery determine our self-image. We crave the applause and seek to build our image on it.

If we do not measure up to man-made standards, we are labelled as failures. We swallow the opinions of men and build our identities on that. There are many who walk around with crushed self-esteem because someone had spoken a false identity over them. There are many crushed dreams because people have branded others according to their standards.

YOU MUST BE BORN AGAIN

Nicodemus, a man of stature in the Jewish community, approached Jesus privately and acknowledged that Jesus must have come from God evidenced by the godly miracles he performed. The identity of Nicodemus in society was a wealthy, learned prince of the Jews. The response of Jesus baffled this ruler of the Jews. Jesus told Nicodemus that one needs to be born again to experience life with God.

"There was a man of the Pharisees named Nicodemus, a ruler of the Jews. This man came to Jesus by night and said to Him, "Rabbi, we know that You are a teacher come from God; for no one can do these signs that You do unless God is with him."

Jesus answered and said to him, "Most assuredly, I say to you, unless one is born again, he cannot see the kingdom of God."

Nicodemus said to Him, "How can a man be born when he is old? Can he enter a second time into his mother's womb and be born?"

Jesus answered, "Most assuredly, I say to you, unless one is born of water and the Spirit, he cannot enter the kingdom of God. That which is born of the flesh is flesh, and that which is born of the Spirit is spirit. Do not marvel that I said to you, 'You must be born again.' The wind blows where it wishes, and you hear the sound of it, but cannot tell where it comes from and where it goes. So is everyone who is born of the Spirit." John 3:1-8

To be born again is to take on a completely new identity. All humans walk around with an identity which falls short of our true identity. Unless you are born again and reconnected to your source, you operate under 'the law of sin and death.' The land of the dead is populated by the dead. The primary identity of anyone on this land is that they are dead. If you walk in this land, you are the walking dead; if you laugh, you are the laughing dead; if you growl, you are the growling dead.

There is a village in Northern Ghana known as Witches Village. This village is populated by people who have been branded witches by the fetish priests of the region. Everyone who lives in the village bears the primary identity of a witch. There are tall and short witches, educated and uneducated witches, rich and poor witches. Unfortunately, these are false identities imposed by deceiving demonic spirits.

In an ignorant, 'survival of the fittest' world, the 'fittest' rules and decides who is who. The fetish priest, through incantations, is able to confer the identity of a witch on anyone he chooses. It is no surprise that, in that patriarchal community of Northern Ghana, all the 'witches' living in this village are women. Most of the fetish priests are men. Women, therefore, become victims. Men also face their own identity crisis as society imposes its own identity on them. You could be labelled a weak or strong man. Society can identify you as a failure or a success. Your disability or suffering could be your identity.

Elizabeth, before she gave birth to John the Baptist, bore the identity of 'the barren woman.'

She did not have any children, so the perception of society had become her identity. Fortunately, that was not her true identity. God had chosen her for a special assignment – to be the mother of John, who was to prepare the way for the coming of Jesus Christ. His identity was 'the greatest of all prophets' before Jesus Christ. When Angel Gabriel appeared to Mary to announce her as God's choice to bring forth the Saviour of the world, he informed her of the conception of John by Elizabeth.

Now indeed, Elizabeth your relative has also conceived a son in her old age; and this is now the sixth month for her who was called barren. For with God nothing will be impossible." Luke 1:36-37

Jesus describing John to his disciples said:

For I say to you, among those born of women there is not a greater prophet than John the Baptist; but he who is least in the kingdom of God is greater than he." John 7:28

Though sin had plunged the world into darkness and ignorance, Jesus Christ came to pay the price for the sins of the world. He served the sentence of death so that we could be plucked out of darkness and ignorance. He has made available to us a new identity – children of God. However, this is not an imposed identity but one that we choose for ourselves. He has offered everyone the opportunity to be born again by God if they so wished. When you are born again, your old identity dies as you put on a new identity and become part of the family of God.

"Therefore, if anyone is in Christ, he is a new creation; old things have passed away; behold, all things have become new." 1 Corinthians 5:17

The only qualification for being born again into the family of God is to receive Jesus Christ. You receive Jesus Christ by acknowledging Him as the Son of God who has come to pay the price for the sin of the world. He faced death by crucifixion as payment for all the sins of the world. He defeated death by rising from the dead on the third day. He is now Lord of all things in heaven and on earth. By this singular act, he is able to reconcile everyone who comes to him to God, as part of his family.

{ CHAPTER 5 }

LIKE FATHER LIKE SON

'You are the true son of your father' is a compliment paid to sons who reproduce some good traits of their fathers. Hidden in this expression is the expectation that good fathers must produce good sons. The opposite can also be true. The expression can also be used sarcastically to mean you are as bad as your father. Jesus put it thus:

"Beware of false prophets, who come to you in sheep's clothing, but inwardly they are ravenous wolves. You will know them by their fruits. Do men gather grapes from thornbushes or figs from thistles? Even so, every good tree bears good fruit, but a bad tree bears bad fruit. A good tree cannot bear bad fruit, nor can a bad tree bear good fruit. Every tree that does not bear good fruit is cut down and thrown

into the fire. Therefore by their fruits you will know them." Matthew 7:15-20

God's plan for procreation was through the seed of a father producing 'after his own kind.' The son has to be the exact image of the father. When God created humans, animals, birds, and plants, he put in them seed to enable them produce after their kind.

We can safely conclude from the account of the creation of man, that God started off with the creation of one of each species. In the case of humans and animals, he created male and female. There was a great variety of species, but each was different. It is interesting to note that several thousand years after God created the world and all in it, new species of plants and animals are being discovered by humans.

He did all things according to the good pleasure of his will. This means that he did what pleased him. As much as you cannot put God in a box, he is a God of order. His plan for multiplication has always been through seed producing after its kind.

The theory that one species evolved into another is not supported by any credible evidence. The theory of evolution introduced by Charles Darwin in the nineteenth century puts the age of our earth at about 4.6 billion years old. For a couple of billion years, nothing happened. His theory guesses that life as we know it, started 570 million years with spiders and insects; fish came a few million years later. The plants, forests and humans came 200,000 years ago. There is no real scientific data to back this wild speculation of a theory spanning billions of years.

Scripture says God created the first man, Adam as Adam. He didn't evolve from a monkey. The first monkey was created as a monkey. There may be species that look similar and are of the monkey kind, but they are all different animals. God created one mango tree, not two or ten. He created one orange tree. From these single original creation, God's intention was to populate the earth with more of its kind through seedtime and harvest.

This would ensure that every fruit would have a seed source and also the capacity to produce more fruit through its own seed. This chain has its beginning in God, the originator and creator of all things. In the account of creation by God in Genesis chapter 1, the last thing God created was man. He created man in his image and likeness and put his breath in man. He put man in charge of his creation. Man needed to multiply through his seed in order to exercise dominion over a universe which was also multiplying.

"Then God said, "Let Us make man in Our image, according to Our likeness; let them have dominion over the fish of the sea, over the birds of the air, and over the cattle, over all the earth and over every creeping thing that creeps on the earth." So God created man in His own image; in the image of God He created him; male and female He created them. Then God blessed them, and God said to them, "Be fruitful and multiply; fill the earth and subdue it; have dominion over the fish of the sea, over the birds of the air, and over every living thing that moves on the earth." Genesis 1:26-28

In the third chapter of the gospel of Luke, Luke traces the ancestry of Jesus Christ back to Adam, the first man. In the 38th verse of that chapter, Adam is referred to as the son of God.

The breath of God was the seed of God that made Adam God's son. After God had formed man, he breathed into the nostrils of man and imparted his seed into man.

"And the Lord God formed man of the dust of the ground, and breathed into his nostrils the breath of life; and man became a living being." Genesis 2:7

When an angel appears to Mary to announce that she is going to be pregnant with Jesus Christ who will be called the son of God, Mary responds with surprise as she had not been with any man. The normal process of birth is for a man to release seed into a woman. Mary, therefore, questioned how it was possible for her to give birth as she had not been impregnated with the seed of any man. Jesus Christ was no ordinary man to be produced by the seed of man. He was the son of God. He had to be produced by the seed of God. **God's seed is His Spirit.**

"Then the angel said to her, "Do not be afraid, Mary, for you have found favor with God. And behold, you will conceive in your womb and bring forth a Son, and shall call His name Jesus. He will

be great, and will be called the Son of the Highest; and the Lord God will give Him the throne of His father David. And He will reign over the house of Jacob forever, and of His kingdom there will be no end."

Then Mary said to the angel, "How can this be, since I do not know a man?"

And the angel answered and said to her, "The Holy Spirit will come upon you, and the power of the Highest will overshadow you; therefore, also, that Holy One who is to be born will be called the Son of God." Luke 1:30-35

If Adam had stayed true to his lineage as Jesus did, he would have walked with the same authority that his father God possessed. God gave birth to Adam to be just like him. He expected Adam to produce sons who would be just like Adam and by natural lineage, just like God. **If Adam had not broken covenant through disobedience, God's bloodline would have run through all people everywhere as God's nature would have naturally passed on from father to son through the generations.**

The result would have been that the wisdom of God would have naturally passed on to men who would use it to rule the rest of God's creation, bringing order to the world. If this flow of God's nature had not been broken by Adam through disobedience, God's peace would have dominated the world instead of the confusion and disorder we see today.

Unfortunately, Adam kicked the spirit of God out of his life by wilfully disobeying God. By disobeying God, Adam was turning his back on the love and wisdom of a father. He was on his own. With the absence of the spirit of God in Adam's life, there was a break of the father-son covenant between Adam and God. This meant that Adam had rejected God as his only source of wisdom and direction. He was now vulnerable to demonic influence. He had unwittingly replaced the solid and faithful fatherhood of God with the uncertainty of a life without God. The devil had indirectly become his God. In a world he knew very little about, that was a tragic decision.

Some countries in the world today, including the United States of America and the United

Kingdom, allow children to legally divorce their parents. This means that their parents cease to be their parents by the direction of the law courts.

The first parental divorce in history was by Adam when he rejected God as father through disobedience. In a dark and confused world, it is possible for some parents to be so unfit as parents that children could be better off without them. It is, however, strange to divorce God, the source of all wisdom and truth; the embodiment of love. His purpose is to share all that he has with his children.

"Do you not know that to whom you present yourselves slaves to obey, you are that one's slaves whom you obey, whether of sin leading to death, or of obedience leading to righteousness? But God be thanked that though you were slaves of sin, yet you obeyed from the heart that form of doctrine to which you were delivered. And having been set free from sin, you became slaves of righteousness." Romans 6:16-18

Who you choose to obey becomes your father by choice. If you choose God as your father, you line yourself up with truth and walk in righteousness. If on the other hand, you choose not to walk with God, you are exposed to the manipulation and deception of the devil.

When Jesus Christ appeared on the scene, one of the things that baffled the Jews and religious leaders of his day was his claim of God as his father. The Jews also claimed God as their father through the covenant he made with their ancestor Abraham. However, they didn't make this claim with much confidence. They had departed so far from the ways of God that they hardly knew Him.

The confidence and authority of Jesus completely undermined the claim of these religious leaders and Pharisees of God as their father. This contrast is made clear in a conversation Jesus had with the religious leaders in John chapter 8:

"I know that you are Abraham's descendants, but you seek to kill Me, because My word has no place in you. I speak what I have seen with My Father, and you do what you have seen with your father."

They answered and said to Him, "Abraham is our father."

Jesus said to them, "If you were Abraham's children, you would do the works of Abraham. But now you seek to kill Me, a Man who has told you the truth which I heard from God. Abraham did not do this. You do the deeds of your father."

Then they said to Him, "We were not born of fornication; we have one Father—God."

Jesus said to them, "If God were your Father, you would love Me, for I proceeded forth and came from God; nor have I come of Myself, but He sent Me. Why do you not understand My speech? Because you are not able to listen to My word. You are of your father the devil, and the desires of your father you want to do. He was a murderer from the beginning, and does not stand in the truth, because there is no truth in him. When he speaks a lie, he speaks from his own resources, for he is a liar and the father of it. But because I tell the truth, you do not believe Me. Which of you convicts Me of sin? And if I tell the truth, why do you not believe Me? He who is of God hears God's words; therefore you do not hear, because you are not of God." John 8:37-47

Jesus proved his identity as the Son of God through the glory of the father he displayed. He taunted his opponents about their desire to murder him and the lies they told as representative of their father, the devil. By the fruit of the son, you know who his father is.

When Philip, one of the disciples of Jesus, asked him to show them the father, Jesus responded that when you see him Jesus, you have seen the father. In other words, 'like father like son.' In the same way, when God becomes your father, you are transformed to be like him. As he is, so you are. Your identity is changed. You are now a child of God and must operate in the freedom your new identity gives to you.

Now the Lord is the Spirit; and where the Spirit of the Lord is, there is liberty. But we all, with unveiled face, beholding as in a mirror the glory of the Lord, are being transformed into the same image from glory to glory, just as by the Spirit of the Lord. 2 Corinthians 3:17-18

CHAPTER 6

THE SPIRIT OF REJECTION

The spirit of rejection is the demonic spirit operating behind all feelings of loneliness and depression. This spirit has been in operation from the beginning when man, through disobedience, cut himself off from God.

God created man to be in a loving relationship with God himself. Adam wilfully stepped out of this relationship through disobedience. Though it was man, who through sin, kicked God out of his life, man still blamed God for his predicament. Children get into a mess and blame their parents for failing to rescue them. Man knew that God was almighty and could bring him back into blessing, so he blamed God for not rescuing him in his struggle. It is not uncommon to hear people blame God for the sicknesses and disasters of this world. People make comments like: "If God was really there, why is there so much injustice in the world? Why do innocent children die?"

God has been and will always be there, but the world has ignored him. The world without God operates under the 'wisdom' of man. The wisdom of man operates under a system of experimentation, 'trial and error' and past experiences. The world without God is cut off from the wisdom of God. God by creating Adam in his image and likeness and breathing life into him, intended to make Adam his son, a true heir of all God's attributes. God intended to use Adam as a channel of truth to all creation. As Adam himself produced fruit after his kind, they would also inherit the same attributes he had inherited from God.

This unbroken chain of inherited truth would have eliminated ignorance and the search for solutions through experimentation. God's word would have prevailed instead of man's word. God's word is light and life. God's word is true and just. God's word is wise and a guide for our actions. God's word creates and brings peace.

"Your word is a lamp to my feet
And a light to my path.
I have sworn and confirmed
That I will keep Your righteous judgments." Psalm
119:105-106

"Is not My word like a fire?" says the Lord,
"And like a hammer that breaks the rock in pieces?
Jeremiah 23:29

"In the beginning was the Word, and the Word was
with God, and the Word was God. He was in the
beginning with God. All things were made through
Him, and without Him nothing was made that was
made. In Him was life, and the life was the light of
men. And the light shines in the darkness, and the
darkness did not comprehend it." John 1:1-5

Rejection is to feel unwanted. When a trusted
relationship is lost, one feels rejected. When the
covenant relationship between God and man was
broken through sin, both man and God would
have felt rejected.

God did not create man as a slave. He created
man in his image and likeness. He gave man
freewill to make free choices. If man therefore

rejects God's love and submits to the authority of another, it is a rejection of God. God expresses this sentiment when the people of Israel approach the prophet Samuel and demand a king. When Samuel approaches God with this request from the people, this was God's response:

"And the Lord said to Samuel, "Heed the voice of the people in all that they say to you; for they have not rejected you, but they have rejected Me, that I should not reign over them." 1 Samuel 8:7

God rejected is knowledge rejected. The quest for knowledge can be painstaking and frustrating. However, man has been able to acquire some knowledge through the grace of and the working brain that God has given to us as humans, and the length of time that mankind has existed. Progress in medicine, science and communication have made our lives less troublesome. Yet the fact that we fall short of God's ideal truth leaves many questions unanswered.

Because we are created in God's image, our inner man craves for perfection, yet the ordinary man falls far short of perfection. This creates a sense of helplessness which makes us feel lonely. We are created in the image and likeness of God but operating far below our potential.

It was for this reason that Jesus came: To re-connect us to our position of acceptance. Anyone who would accept this free invitation of God's love buys a ticket to acceptance and companionship and says goodbye to rejection and loneliness. Acceptance has replaced rejection.

Jesus came to reconcile everyone back to the father. He has come as a Son of the Father - God. Everything the father has is his and everything the father is, He is. Spiritual orphans can now become sons of God through Him.

"For it pleased the Father that in Him all the fullness should dwell, and by Him to reconcile all things to Himself, by Him, whether things on earth or things in heaven, having made peace through the blood of His cross.

And you, who once were alienated and enemies in your mind by wicked works, yet now He has reconciled in the body of His flesh through death, to present you holy, and blameless, and above reproach in His sight— if indeed you continue in the faith, grounded and steadfast, and are not moved away from the hope of the gospel which you heard, which was preached to every creature under heaven, of which I, Paul, became a minister." Colossians 1:19-23

VICTIMS OF REJECTION

Every person without God has a sense of insecurity and rejection. Our separation from God is the mother of all rejection. There are however other life events that have caused further rejection in many people. The following paragraphs are true accounts of people who faced serious rejection and loneliness. Thankfully, they have all received the solution of reconciliation with God through Jesus Christ and joyfully give their testimony to help others receive their deliverance. Their names have been changed to protect their identity.

JOHN'S STORY

John is an entrepreneur who has built a successful business with an annual turnover of millions of pounds. He lived comfortably in a beautiful home with his wife and two children. To the casual observer, he is the personification of success; one you aspired to but yet he felt empty inside. Though he tried to smile with confidence and keep up the appearance of well-being, he was a broken man inside. There was a 'father' void in his spirit. His salesman father was rarely at home because the nature of his work involved travelling around the United States. Even though he brought John all sorts of gifts and material things which he bought for him from his travels, these things never compensated for his absence. Since his father was not present at any of his school functions, the presence of other fathers made John feel lonely and resentful towards his father. Over a period of time, a spirit of rejection created a deep hole in John's spirit. This affected his academic work, and he performed poorly at exams. He put his energy into business and succeeded financially, but the void was still there.

John got married and had his own family, yet this heritage of loneliness had made him very possessive and overprotective of his family. Anything that competed for the affection of his wife and children was an enemy. Finally,

John's deliverance came when his wife became a Christian through some friends. At first, he was very suspicious of the conversion of his wife, but after observing the positive change and freedom that faith in Jesus Christ brought to his wife, it had an impact on him. He then started attending Christian meetings with his wife and eventually gave his heart to Jesus Christ.

John became part of the men's group in his church where the topic of rejection came up in one of their discussion nights. He found out he was not alone. Most men have experienced rejection from their fathers which they, in turn, have passed on to their sons. Most men find it difficult to express their pain. Many would conveniently hide their vulnerability in burying their heads in work, alcohol and drug abuse or anger and bullying.

Thankfully, John became a part of a group that was ready to be frank and open about rejection and loneliness. Through the support of his fellow men, John submitted to the inviting arms of Father God. By the study of God's word and prayer and an understanding of the complete fatherhood of God, he was completely delivered. He was able to forgive his father. He has now dedicated his life to helping other people to be set free from rejection and loneliness. John says he receives so much joy from his ministry of bringing deliverance to the lonely. His business has continued to grow because he is more relaxed as he has made God a partner in everything he does.

My prayer for you, as you read this book, is that Almighty God, the father of all things will remove every heartache and loneliness from your life. May your understanding of God's love be deepened that you would run into His waiting arms to obtain mercy in your time of need.

Many are experiencing a new lease of life as they have willingly embraced Father God and submitted to the bathing of His Spirit.

PETER'S STORY

Peter lived with his two sisters and mother. His parents divorced when he was five years old. He grew close to his maternal uncle in his search for a father figure. He was sexually abused at the age of ten by this uncle. This confused him and greatly affected him emotionally. He was confused about his sexuality as a teenager. He got into drugs and ended up in a psychiatric hospital. At a rehabilitation centre, he met Christians and through their interactions with him, he eventually gave his life to Jesus Christ.

Though the leaders of Peter's new church were welcoming and accepting, his own sense of insecurity plagued him. He thought other church members were disapproving of him. He would enjoy the prayers, the songs and the words of encouragement coming from the pulpit but was suspicious of the actions of individual members of the congregation. He misinterpreted encouraging comments from others as patronising. For the first three years of his conversion, he attended church services regularly but also had bouts of depression and alcohol binges. He had ballooned in weight because of his medication and was extremely self-conscious.

His faithfulness in church attendance paid off. One day a guest preacher called him out to pray for him. As hands were laid on him, he felt weak at the knees and lost consciousness. When he revived a few minutes later, he knew he was a different man. He felt light, joyful and confident. Everyone and everything around him was so lovely. The burden of spite and pain he carried in his heart had been lifted. He knew he was free. The Holy Spirit had invaded his soul and lifted his burden. From that day, he began to know the love and peace of God which is beyond understanding. He has grown in this knowledge and no longer has a need for medication or intoxication to get rid of depression. Today, Peter is married with two sons of his own, bringing up his children in the admonition of the Lord.

JO'S STORY

Jo is an exuberant, bright lady. When you meet her, the joy flowing from her is infectious. Jo says she wished she had a Dad who had stopped her from dating older men when she was only 16. She had boasted that she preferred older men as they were more mature. She really enjoyed her relationship with this one particular man. According to her, she felt very secure in his arms. After all, he was only 32 and gave her money and attention. Unfortunately, this 'kind' man abandoned her when he made her pregnant. Jo said she was so disappointed and felt rejected. She hated herself and ended up in prostitution and petty crime. Her motivation for prostitution was not only to make money, but it also made her feel wanted. She explains that in a strange sort of way, prostitution made her feel powerful over men. This was her coping mechanism for her rejection.

Finding Jesus Christ brought deliverance to Jo. Today she ministers to those in prostitution, setting them free. Many of these former prostitutes have similar stories like hers to tell.

SANTOSH'S STORY

Santosh admits that he met Jesus Christ when he was behind bars and he is now so free that he has forgiven his alcoholic and abusive father. Though he is serving a life sentence for murder, he is so free from guilt that he speaks about Jesus Christ to other inmates and has helped others to be set free from the bondage of rejection and guilt. Many of the inmates in the prison have come from broken homes and are oppressed by the spirit of rejection. One thing Santosh is sure about is how deeply the absence of a responsible father affected his life. As he enjoys the faithfulness of God as his father, his pain and loneliness have been erased. He is, therefore, able to confidently point a way out of this misery to other sufferers.

The spirit of rejection can even attack a baby in the womb. A pregnant woman who feels rejected can pass on this rejection to the baby she is carrying. Rejection is a spirit and can be passed on from the spirit of the mother to that of the unborn child. Rejection could happen when a parent unwittingly compares two siblings and elevates one above the other.

Rejection is love rebuffed; a trust betrayed, a covenant broken, an expectation dashed. This leads to a sense of total betrayal. When your peace is disturbed, demonic spirits exploit your confusion by oppressing you with dejection, anger and rebellion. Rejection leads to dejection which leads to anger then rebellion.

The only antidote to rejection is acceptance. God, through the sacrificial love of Jesus Christ on the Cross of Calvary, has provided a complete acceptance package which everyone has to access and make their own. Everyone needs deliverance from separation from God. The spirit of rejection operates in every person till it is destroyed by being accepted into the household of God. Your first step to obtaining complete deliverance from any rejection and loneliness is to accept Jesus Christ into your life.

I invite you to pray this prayer sincerely:

Dear Father God, you are the ultimate father. You are God of the whole earth. I thank you for your love for me. Lord Jesus Christ, I thank you for your act of love by which you died on the Cross of Calvary for my sins so I could be reconciled to the heavenly father. I accept your invitation and turn from my own ways. Come into my life and fill the void in my life. Amen.

CHAPTER 7

WAKE UP MAN!

"Then Jesus said to them, "All of you will be made to stumble because of Me this night, for it is written: 'I will strike the Shepherd, And the sheep will be scattered.'" Mark 14:27

When leadership is lost, followers are confused. Men were created as family leaders. When manhood is lost, the family becomes weak. When the strength of the family is attacked, the foundation of society is shaken.

Scripture tells us that God first created man. He then created a woman out of man. Children are produced out of the union of man and woman. That settles the leadership question. The man is the leader and seed carrier of the family. The man cannot produce fruit by himself. He needs the woman to receive the seed, nurture it and bring forth fruit.

The position of leadership for man is not a position of superiority. It is a position of responsibility. When the devil attacks leadership, his intention is to kill vision or seed. The devil has been unrelenting in his attack on the leadership of men in the family. This started right from the Garden of Eden when Satan in the form of a serpent made an attack on the leadership of man through the deception of Eve, his wife.

Paul says in his letter to Timothy that Eve was deceived, but Adam was not. Adam was just disobedient because the order not to eat of the fruit was given to Adam. Adam was supposed to drive that vision. His wife just offered the sin to him, and he ate it. In that move of disobedience, the whole family was cut off from God. His disobedience brought a curse on his family and subsequently on all of us, their descendants.

If Eve had eaten of the fruit alone, Adam could have stood in the gap before God and pleaded for mercy on Eve's behalf. That is what Jesus presently does on behalf of the Church. When the father relinquishes the responsibility of leadership, the family is exposed to attacks of the enemy. This is why restoration of fatherhood is essential to revival in the Church. Paul is not being chauvinistic when he affirms the position of men in the conduct of affairs in the Church.

"And I do not permit a woman to teach or to have authority over a man, but to be in silence. For Adam was formed first, then Eve. And Adam was not deceived, but the woman being deceived, fell into transgression. Nevertheless she will be saved in childbearing if they continue in faith, love, and holiness, with self-control." 1 Timothy 2:12-15

God's natural order of dispensing authority is: God – Man – Wife – Children. When man separated himself from God, he cut himself off from the natural wisdom and love of God. Without the attributes of God, man's ordained position as leader was greatly undermined. Authority is received from a more authoritative source. The final authority in all things is God. With God out of the equation, man had to create his own authority. This led to unjust, self-serving impositions and laws which were favourable to men but unfavourable to women and children. Man has used his muscle to bully his way into self-preservation. **When the order of God was disturbed, it became survival of the fittest. The weaker animals became food for the stronger.**

Some communities in the world still deny formal education to their women because the laws are made by men. I heard a senator in an African country openly admit on the floors of parliament that it would be a disaster to give women the same rights as men. His fear was that men would lose their position of authority if women were given the same opportunities. This is the voice of fear and self-preservation.

Many communities in the world today practise polygamy. Men are allowed to have multiple wives but for the woman to do the same is considered a taboo. The Bible says: "Do to others as you would like them to do to you." It also tells us "To love others as we love ourselves."

Obeying these commands are near impossible without the help of God. The helplessness of humans in a world they know very little about makes them vulnerable. When people are afraid, they will protect themselves with whatever weapon they have. A drowning man would hold on to whatever, even if it means dragging others down to drown with him. **Disorder always promotes slavery: economic and social slavery.**

When true leadership is missing, there is confusion. This has been our curse as humans. False leadership has replaced true leadership. Leadership has been stolen by the eloquent and the rich. Politicians, money-men and the media are the real shapers of general thinking in our society today.

This is not how God intended it to be. God's plan was that real authority would be received from heaven which would release peace and order on the earth. The first man, Adam, had rejected God, lost his authority and plunged the world into disorder and chaos. The agenda of the Son, Jesus Christ, was to pay the penalty of death for Adam's sin. Adam's sin plunged all of us, his descendants, into sin and death. We were separated from God into a life of ignorance and darkness.

The mission of Jesus was to reconcile the world to God and restore the order of heaven on earth. This is the only hope for mankind. Isaiah, prophesying about this mission of Jesus Christ 700 years before it happened, put it thus:

"For unto us a Child is born,
Unto us a Son is given;
And the government will be upon His shoulder.
And His name will be called
Wonderful, Counselor, Mighty God,
Everlasting Father, Prince of Peace.
Of the increase of His government and peace
There will be no end,
Upon the throne of David and over His kingdom,
To order it and establish it with judgment and justice
From that time forward, even forever.
The zeal of the Lord of hosts will perform this."
Isaiah 9:6-7

Jesus would come as a human being, born as a normal child. Yet, this was no ordinary child. He was the son of God. What this meant was that he had the image, likeness and attributes of God. His attributes are mentioned as Wonderful, Counsellor, Mighty God, Everlasting Father and the Prince of Peace. He was to reign as a king like David. His kingdom would be established forever. He was mandated to bring Order and Justice on the earth. That is exactly what the earth needs today. The Prince of Peace brings justice and peace. Isaiah elaborates on the attributes of Jesus and the resulting peace of his coming in Isaiah chapter 11 and verses 1-9:

"There shall come forth a Rod from the stem of Jesse,
And a Branch shall grow out of his roots.
The Spirit of the Lord shall rest upon Him,
The Spirit of wisdom and understanding,
The Spirit of counsel and might,
The Spirit of knowledge and of the fear of the Lord.
His delight is in the fear of the Lord,
And He shall not judge by the sight of His eyes,
Nor decide by the hearing of His ears;
But with righteousness He shall judge the poor,
And decide with equity for the meek of the earth;
He shall strike the earth with the rod of His mouth,
And with the breath of His lips He shall slay the wicked.
Righteousness shall be the belt of His loins,

And faithfulness the belt of His waist.
"The wolf also shall dwell with the lamb,
The leopard shall lie down with the young goat,
The calf and the young lion and the fatling together;
And a little child shall lead them.
The cow and the bear shall graze;
Their young ones shall lie down together;
And the lion shall eat straw like the ox.
The nursing child shall play by the cobra's hole,
And the weaned child shall put his hand in the viper's den.
They shall not hurt nor destroy in all My holy mountain,
For the earth shall be full of the knowledge of the Lord
As the waters cover the sea."

With the right authority in place, even avowed enemies would be at peace. The wolf and the lamb will dwell together; the leopard and the young goat will lie next to each other in peace. The calf and the young lion shall be together without fear. Interestingly, a little child shall lead them. That is the order of God. **If humans would submit to God, all animals would submit to humans, even children.**

If men would take their rightful place in submission to God, it would be easy for wives and children to submit. Authority, lovingly dispensed, is delightful to submit to. Just as Moses stood between God and Israel and Jesus stands between the Father and the world, men are called to be the priests and prophets of their families. God's desire is that men would stand in the gap for their communities.

"I desire therefore that the men pray everywhere, lifting up holy hands, without wrath and doubting;"
1 Timothy 2:8

God originally created man to lead and gave him the physique and attributes to lead from the front. The woman was created to be a helper to man's vision. As expressed earlier, this does not in any way belittle the position of the woman. As someone wisely put it: The man builds a house, the woman creates a home. The man's position of leadership is a position of service. Jesus admonished his disciples that leadership in his kingdom is service to others.

In a fallen world, weak men have necessitated leadership from strong women. When women pray more than men, they are bound to hear more from God than men would. They would walk more in the power of the Holy Spirit than men would. Walking more in the power of the Holy Spirit means they would be stronger, wiser and more envisioned than the men. In the midst of weak men, strong women rise to leadership.

My call out is that men should arise and take up the position of responsibility entrusted to them by God. One man, Jesus, stood in the gap for the whole world. He has entrusted his power on earth to His Church which he calls His Body. The Church must be a father to the whole community.

By the anointing of the Holy Spirit, the Christ-like men in the Church have the capacity to father all in the community, and the Christ-like women have the capacity to mother all in the community. Not all children have a responsible and present father. Some fathers are fathers in name only. Not every woman has a husband, and not all men would get married. Jesus Christ did not have a wife, and we know from Scripture that the Apostle Paul was never married. However, we have no greater father of our faith than Jesus Christ, and Paul remains one of the greatest fathers of the church. Jesus said that he did what pleased his father, so his father was always with him. Paul said he had fought a good fight of faith and was awaiting his crown of glory. Both were confident that they had successfully stood between God and man and accomplished their assignment of service.

Everyman joined to Father God, has the capacity to operate in the same authority Jesus and Paul operated in. This is because the flow from God has been restored. The starting point for a close relationship with God is the place of prayer and intercession. Who you pray for is who you can receive a message for. Every man can stand in the gap for his family. If the man takes back his position as head of the family and community, restored order will bring restored peace.

Destroy the Head and the Body will Crumble

Scripture tells us that Satan was an angel created by God. He grew ambitious and rebelled against

God. He was thrown out from the presence of God. Displaced from his station before God, his abode became outer darkness. Twisted and bitter but unable to revenge directly on God, he turned on God's most cherished possession, humans. His main target has been the leadership of man. If he could demolish the leadership role of man, the rest of creation would scatter.

As is the nature of the devil, he goes about this subtly and clandestinely. He knows if he could separate man away from God, the confidence of man would be hit, and he would not be able to lead the rest of creation. The sure way of separation from God is walking in disobedience to him. When Satan wanted to attack Adam, he did not go directly to Adam but went through the weaker, Eve. After deceiving Eve, the woman was able to recruit Adam into disobedience. Guilt made Adam very fearful. Even when God called out to him after he ate the forbidden fruit, he could not face God. He felt naked and condemned. He knew whom he had disobeyed. His moment of indiscretion had cost him the loving relationship of a father.

The many wars that have been fought through the ages have done great damage to men. Many men have been killed in wars, and this has been one of the reasons cited by Islam to allow men to marry up to four wives. "Wars have caused a shortage of men, so allowing multiple wives for men, would enable more women to enjoy marriage."

Men who survive the war are left largely traumatised. They observe such inhumane action in war that their souls are badly wounded. They have lost close friends and associates and others are badly wounded. The extreme fear and anger experienced by soldiers in war can lead to brain damage. It is not uncommon to see men return from war with severe psychiatric problems. Alcoholism and drug addiction are quite common among former warriors. Some resort to reclusive lifestyles, walking in guilt and condemnation.

A smart and jolly friend of mine would suddenly suffer bouts of depression and panic attacks. We traced this to his participation in the Sierra Leonean civil war which went for over ten years in the last decade of the 20th century. He had seen family members murdered, maimed and raped.

He had been involved in demonic initiations to 'empower' him to fight. For his young age, he had seen too much. This plays back in his mind every now and then and plunges him into uncontrollable panic.

There is solution to every trauma one has suffered that makes them vulnerable. That is the purpose of this book. You can be delivered and made whole again. My friend has been delivered by the Blood of Jesus and strengthened by the Word of God and brings deliverance to other men. The enemy has used wars to weaken the authority of men.

The first and second world wars greatly undermined the confidence of men to offer leadership to society. The many ongoing pockets of war between and within nations have turned men from being symbols of stability to becoming refugees. Men are fleeing their own land and begging to be accommodated in other lands.

Satan is ultimately the architect of all wars. It is he who orchestrated the first rebellion and plunged the world into disorder, competition and the fight for supremacy.

Adam was influenced to start the first rebellion against God. He was cut off from the leadership and wisdom of God. He had his own children and became a leader without proper authority; a navigator without a map. He became such a terrible father that his first son, Cain, killed his second son Abel out of envy. From the moment man left the peaceful presence of God, the strength and leadership of man were misdirected to strife and contention with one another. The devil has exploited this rivalry to end the lives of many men and further undermine the confidence of men.

Jesus has come to restore order. We can come under the authority of Father God. As we receive from him, we can also become fathers of orderly children. We can pass on the peace we receive from our heavenly Father to our sons.

Chapter 8

AUTHORITY IN THE CHURCH

"Now, therefore, you are no longer strangers and foreigners, but fellow citizens with the saints and members of the household of God, having been built on the foundation of the apostles and prophets, Jesus Christ Himself being the chief cornerstone, in whom the whole building, being fitted together, grows into a holy temple in the Lord, in whom you also are being built together for a dwelling place of God in the Spirit." Ephesians 2:19-22

God's purpose for the creation of man was to have a family for himself. This is why he created man in his image and likeness and breathed his life into man. If the first man, Adam, had not turned his back on God, God's ideal would be that the whole world would be his family. He would be a father to all, protecting, providing and leading all.

Unfortunately, Adam rejected God through disobedience and God had to embark on a rescue plan. Humans created in his image were a lost family who needed rescue, so God sent Jesus Christ to the rescue. Jesus has paid the price of death for the disobedience of the first man Adam. Through this, he has laid the foundation for the return of the whole world back to the family of God. The only requirement for anyone to return into the family of God is a willingness to return.

The only path for this return is Jesus Christ. Jesus said: *"I am the way, the truth, and the life. No one comes to the Father except through Me." (John 14:6)*. The reason why Jesus is the only way is the fact that he is the only one certified as spotless and without sin and therefore worthy to stand before God, and it is only through him that anyone can qualify to appear before God.

Those who respond to this invitation of God to be his children are called the Church, a translation from the Greek word, Ekklesia, which literally means the 'Called out.' Not everyone would say 'yes' to the invitation of God but those who say yes, become part of his family.

The basic family unit of husband wife and children is representative of God's bigger family, the Church. In the 5th chapter of Paul's letter to the Ephesians, as Paul exhorts husbands to love their wives, he draws parallels with Christ's relationship with the Church. The Church is called the Bride of Christ. It is also called the Body of Christ. Scripture says that the husband and wife are joined together to become one flesh so is Christ one with his Church.

"For we are members of His body, of His flesh and of His bones. "For this reason a man shall leave his father and mother and be joined to his wife, and the two shall become one flesh." This is a great mystery, but I speak concerning Christ and the church." Ephesians 5:30-32.

In the world today, God's concept of family is not working as intended by the creator. Truth be told, the power of family is not being encouraged as it should be. With the absence of the comfort of family as purposed by God, the saying: "Each one for himself and God for us all" is playing before our eyes. Competitiveness resulting in loneliness is the order of the day. Fathers have lost the confidence to take up their leadership role in the family.

As the family unit has been in disarray because of the loss of the leadership authority of the father, so has the Church been plagued with division as the office of the Apostle has been ignored or abused along the years. Scripture tells us that the Church is built on the foundation of the apostles and prophets with Jesus Christ as the corner stone.

The apostles are the fathers of the church. They act as the foundation of the church by the mandate they have received from Jesus Christ. **As the apostle is the father of the church, so is the father the apostle of the family.** They are vision carriers who must be followed.

God is restoring fatherhood in the church by restoring the true office of the Apostle. When the true office of the apostle is restored, there shall be unity and God's order in the church. As the church is strengthened by the restoration of the apostolic office, this authority will naturally flow from the church to the basic family unit. Fathers will become fathers again. Men will no longer be afraid to take on the responsibility as vision carriers, protectors and providers. When God is your source, it is a joy to serve as you are endowed with all provision for service.

When order is restored in the Church, there shall be a great manifestation of the Holy Spirit as in the first church.

It is an indictment on our society today that, as I write this book, the Metropolitan Police Commissioner for London who is the topmost Police officer in the United Kingdom is a woman. As much as I think men and women are equal and believe that the Present Commissioner is probably the most qualified in the circumstance, I also think that we the men in the UK should bow our heads in shame. Men are built to protect the family and be the primary source of discipline. When men act weak, women would be foolish to sit down and suffer the consequence, doing nothing.

A pastor friend just called today to inform me that a groom had pulled out of a wedding scheduled to happen tomorrow. This wedding had taken a year to plan. This sudden disruption to the dream of his bride and families involved is not due to any misconduct on the part of the bride, but just indecision and absence of strength of character on the part of the man. This is what many of our men, who are supposed to lead as fathers, have been reduced to. They enjoy relationships but shy away from responsibility. The sense of responsibility and confidence is absent because they feel inadequate.

God has seen this and is empowering his Church in these last days with the quality of leadership that our society needs, to align itself to the original intention of God. The Church is returning to its apostolic roots and releasing a clear direction to the world. Find your place in it by submitting to the apostolic authority of the Church.

Though the numbers in the early church were small, they had the reputation of 'turning the whole world upside down.' Today's church has greater numbers and more miracles in terms of volume, yet it has less impact because it is scattered and divided. God has promised in his word that the glory of the latter house is going to be greater than the glory of the former. This means that we who are alive today, haven't seen anything yet. We are going to see greater than we have ever seen or heard. Today's church must, therefore, prepare itself for an impact that will be greater than that of the early church.

With the restoration of the apostolic ministry in the church, true fatherhood is being restored in the church, bringing it to the place of power. When the altar is built, and sacrifice is laid in order, fire comes from the presence of God to consume it.

The five-fold leadership offices do not function effectively till the apostolic office is in place. The scripture at the beginning of this chapter shows that the offices of the apostle and prophet are the foundation of the church with Jesus Christ as the cornerstone. It is the five-fold ministry gifts that will bring the church to the place of perfection.

"And He Himself gave some to be apostles, some prophets, some evangelists, and some pastors and teachers, for the equipping of the saints for the work of ministry, for the edifying of the body of Christ, till we all come to the unity of the faith and of the knowledge of the Son of God, to a perfect man, to the measure of the stature of the fullness of Christ;" Ephesians 4:11-13.

THE APOSTOLIC MINISTRY

The apostolic ministry is a foundational ministry. This means that the apostle is the starting point of a unique move of God. Not only does he start this move, but he also supervises and maintains it. The foundation stones of a building are laid at the start of the building, and they also carry the building ensuring firm rooting. That is the work of the apostle.

When Jesus chose his first twelve disciples, they were the foundation of a movement of disciples. We know in Luke 10:1 that it came to a point, after the first twelve, when he commissioned seventy disciples to move in his name and authority. In Acts chapter 2, the Holy Spirit from heaven fell on

120 disciples, empowering them to introduce the power of God to the whole world. This gradual progression in numbers has resulted in the many millions who call themselves disciples of Jesus Christ today. The foundation of this great move is still the original twelve apostles with Jesus as the cornerstone.

The Church of Jesus Christ is built on the doctrine of the original apostles. These received from Jesus and passed it on. They had a direct mandate from heaven to visit heaven on earth. This mandate was to be the pillars of the heavenly vision of reconciling the world back to God. They were commissioned to be bridges connecting the created to the creator. They possessed the identity of the created but displayed the authority of the Creator which they received at their commissioning. **Apostles move in great spiritual authority**.

Though there were the foundational twelve with Matthias replacing Judas after the latter's betrayal of Jesus, the office of the apostle did not stop with the first twelve. God would begin new apostolic moves in the growing Church, and these moves were and are driven by apostles. Though we call these apostolic moves new, they are not different from the original vision of God entrusted to the original twelve. However, they are details of God's purpose in building his Church as it moved from one level of glory to greater glory. Apostles are needed to undertake these special assignments in the mind of God, necessary for the maturity of the Church.

The early church had apostles who were not part of the original twelve. Barnabas and Paul are referred to as Apostles by Luke in Acts 14:14. In fact, Paul introduces himself as an apostle chosen by God in his epistles. Paul describes Andronicus and Junias as notable apostles in Romans 16:7. There are other apostles mentioned in the early church in reference to the work they did.

The word 'Apostolos' is the Greek for a 'sent one' or special messenger; a delegate, ambassador or commissioner of Christ. This could, therefore, refer to anyone with a pioneering mandate from heaven. Though with a direct mandate from heaven, the apostle is never an independent worker. The first apostles were completely dependent on the direction of the Holy Spirit and accountable to the Church. Paul in his powerful apostolic ministry deferred to the Church Council in Jerusalem. Timothy, an apostle in his own right, was the spiritual son of the Apostle Paul.

There is a part of the Church that believes that the only true apostles are the original 12 who walked with Jesus Christ. The 12 original apostles are the foundational pillars of the Church. John refers to them in Revelation 21:14 as the twelve foundations of the New Jerusalem. The New Jerusalem is the Bride of Christ, which is the Church.

"Now the wall of the city had twelve foundations, and on them were the names of the twelve apostles of the Lamb." Revelation 21:14

The apostolic ministry, however, is not limited to the first century of the Church. Paul lists the Apostle as one of the five offices, in Ephesians 4:11, needed by the Church. "Their responsibility is to equip God's people to do His work and build up the church, the body of Christ. **This will continue until we all come to such unity in our faith and knowledge of God's Son that we will**

be mature in the Lord, measuring up to the full and complete standard of Christ." (NLT).

As the maturity of the Church is not complete, the apostolic ministry is needed in today's church to lead and carry the burden of the building of the Church. The Apostle is one, who through a heavenly mandate, has the strength to endure the challenges of a pacesetter (apostolic travail) and is endowed as a mighty warrior of Christ to stand in the position of a father in the church.

The Church needs fathers who are wise, patient and walk in great authority to execute the vision of the master in reconciling the world to God and preparing a perfect bride for His Son, Jesus Christ.

The end time harvest is going to be great and quick. This harvest is going to require several mighty men of the gospel. King David could not have ascended the throne of Israel without his mighty warriors who were ready to die for the cause and in so doing, were rewarded with enviable positions around him in his kingship.

Moses once said that he wished all had the spirit of God and were prophets. How God would be delighted if there were many ready to be mighty men. We must all desire not only to be part of the family of God but to be a special sent one or an apostle, a father in the church around whom God can gather a family of his children for his purpose. There are some who have taken on the title of an apostle for their own selfish ends. Every work of the Lord will be tested by fire. It is important for the Lord to appoint you into an office than for you to arrogate to yourself a title. If you sincerely desire any office and are ready to pay the price, it is yours for the asking. Desire to be a mighty warrior, an apostle of the living God. David said in Psalm 92:

The righteous shall flourish like a palm tree,
He shall grow like a cedar in Lebanon.
Those who are planted in the house of the Lord
Shall flourish in the courts of our God. Psalm
92:12,13

What the Church of Christ is waiting for are apostles who are ready to fearlessly walk in the authority of Jesus Christ in this end time harvest of reconciling the world to God.

What the family of God needs now are fathers who are ready to patiently nurture spiritual children to maturity, fearlessly and skilfully using the word of God to build and protect God's family in a hostile world.

What the army of God desperately requires are mighty warriors like David's mighty warriors, who were ready to confront giants, stand their ground when others are fleeing and ready to fight to the finish.

Every child of God can pay the price to maturity. In fact, normalcy in spiritual walk is to mature from spiritual childhood to becoming a spiritual father. In our physical development, stunted growth is a disability. If we could help it, we would steer away from any disability. Spiritual disability, unlike some physical disabilities, is a choice. The power to grow into spiritual maturity is in our hands. God has completely offered his love and guidance by a blood covenant. We can be apostles, fathers and mighty warriors in his kingdom. Choose what you would be as the world, as we know it, is passing away and being replaced by the kingdom of God. Strive to be a father in the kingdom.

CHAPTER 9

FINAL WORD

The world is constantly getting worse in spite of the relentless effort of people trying to make it better. Over the ages, there have been many strong kings, mighty warriors, inventors, philosophers, religious figures, good-natured men and women, some of whom have tried to make the world a better place. Truth be told, despite advances in science and so-called civilisation, the world seems to be getting worse. 'The good old days' is a popular saying referring to a past which, though not that good, seems better than the present.

The world has been systematically crumbling because of the wrong foundation it operates on. God did not create the world on a bad foundation. **God created the world with Himself as its**

foundation. The rejection of God meant a world without foundation. Any building without a proper foundation is bound to crumble.

Every new person who comes into the world must have a foundation of a father and mother waiting for them. Although in a fallen and ignorant world, this is not always the case. Many fathers and mothers run away from their foundational responsibilities. Some children also reject their foundation. The attempt by men to build a good world without a good foundation is an exercise in futility. The world is collapsing like a building without a foundation.

If God had left us humans to our arrogant, know-all attitude, our ignorance and frustration would eventually wipe us all out. Ignorance, frustration, loneliness and depression are destroying lives around us every day.

A good and loving God would not allow His creation to go through this fruitless existence of stumbling from one calamity to the other. His love for his creation would not allow that. His power has put in place a plan of rescue that cannot fail.

A new foundation has been built. A kingdom built with Jesus Christ as the cornerstone. The same Word of God that man rejected to find himself fatherless has returned to rescue man. It would be foolish for clueless disintegrating man to ignore such a great salvation. The Psalmist prophesying about this day of restoration hundreds of years before it happened said:

"This is the gate of the Lord,
Through which the righteous shall enter.
I will praise You,
For You have answered me,
And have become my salvation.
The stone which the builders rejected
Has become the chief cornerstone.
This was the Lord's doing;
It is marvelous in our eyes.
This is the day the Lord has made;
We will rejoice and be glad in it." Psalm 118:20-24

The Father of the fatherless has come to the rescue. No one needs to be fatherless any longer. What the world had always needed was a father to direct its path; a foundation on which it would rest. That Foundation has come as a father to all who would receive Him.

"Let us therefore come boldly to the throne of grace, that we may obtain mercy and find grace to help in time of need." Hebrews 4:16

God has ordained that those who would so choose to be part of his kingdom would be beautified as a worthy bride of Christ. This is what you would be:

"But you are a chosen generation, a royal priesthood, a holy nation, His own special people, that you may proclaim the praises of Him who called you out of darkness into His marvelous light; who once were not a people but are now the people of God, who had not obtained mercy but now have obtained mercy." 1 Peter 2:9-10

Jesus Christ in his incarnation came to lead a fatherless world back into the arms of a waiting, loving father with arms wide open to receive his long-lost children back. To achieve this, he paid the price of death for sin which separated us from God, our father. Sin and death are defeated foes under the complete authority of Jesus Christ.

When Jesus Christ rose from the dead, he could confidently tell his disciples:

"All authority has been given to Me in heaven and on earth. Go therefore and make disciples of all the nations, baptizing them in the name of the Father and of the Son and of the Holy Spirit, teaching them to observe all things that I have commanded you; and lo, I am with you always, even to the end of the age." Amen. Matthew 28:18-20

Jesus Christ did not only clear the way to the Father of the whole world, but He also destroyed the chains that bound humanity in bondage to fear and destruction. No one has an excuse to live as fatherless orphans any longer. The father of the whole world is waiting to welcome all home.

Many are living as orphans out of ignorance; princes living as paupers. This is why the Almighty Father, through Jesus Christ, has sent each one of us his children, to go out there and tell the world about Him, reconciling a lost and lonely world back to their father. The chains have fallen off, and the prison doors are open. Arise and come boldly to your Father God, who fearfully and wonderfully made you.

"Arise, shine;
For your light has come!
And the glory of the Lord is risen upon you.
For behold, the darkness shall cover the earth,
And deep darkness the people;
But the Lord will arise over you,
And His glory will be seen upon you.
The Gentiles shall come to your light,
And kings to the brightness of your rising.
"Lift up your eyes all around, and see:
They all gather together, they come to you;
Your sons shall come from afar,
And your daughters shall be nursed at your side."
Isaiah 60:1-4

When the head is in place, the body operates right. Jesus as the foundation of the Church is also its leader. He is both the Cornerstone and the Capstone. The Church a movement of his brothers and sisters who have made God their father.

As the spiritual head of the Church, Jesus has appointed human fathers for the church. These are called apostles. The devil has fought the restoration of the office of the Apostle in the church in the same way he has fought every beneficial move of God for mankind. He has deceived, ridiculed and counterfeited. As with all his deceptive moves, he is headed towards failure. The office of the apostle is being restored in God's Church, and this marks a golden age for the church. When the head is in place, the body is envisioned and empowered.

Good fathers are rising to play their leadership role in the family. The devil's agenda of weakening the family by destroying the confidence of fathers is over. Confident fathers, hooked up to the Spirit of God, are rising and leading their families out of the miry clay into the solid, steady and joyful arms of God.

The restoration of fatherhood is the greatest blow to the devil after the death and resurrection of Jesus Christ. Satan knows he has been defeated and humiliated by Jesus Christ. What he has been playing at is to keep humans distracted from the truth through deception and disorder. God's purpose and timing always prevail. Fathers are being restored. This means order and imparted knowledge. It also means the Bridegroom is soon coming for his Bride.

Rejoice. You are part of God's plan. You have a father who is faithful, and He is making you into a faithful father or mother over his creation. Why don't you join me in gratitude to pray this prayer:

Thank you, my Father, for the love with which you created me.
Thank you, Jesus, for the sacrifice you made for my rescue.
Thank you, Holy Spirit for the revelation of the Father you have given to me.
Thank you, God, for empowering me to be a father/mother in your kingdom.
I completely submit to your leadership and moulding.
Strengthen and guide me to be what you created me to be.

I pray God's blessing over you and your household. May the revelation of God's word enlighten and embolden you to live a victorious life in the Name of Jesus.

BE STRONG PUBLICATIONS

Other books by the author, Martin Ossei:

1. The Day Of The Son
2. Death Exposed, Fear Defeated, **Life Forevermore**
3. Be Strong Devotional (Whole Year Daily Reading For Spiritual Strength)

website: www.bestrongpublications.com